Telling the Bees

Telling the Bees

Poems

Cathryn Essinger

Sheila-Na-Gig Editions

Cover art: Shutterstock by Martin Pelanek

ISBN: 9781962405713
Library of Congress Control Number: 2026936809

Sheila-Na-Gig Editions
Russell, KY
Hayley Mitchell Haugen, Editor
www.sheilanagigblog.com

Printed in the United States of America

Acknowledgments

About Place: "I Ask the Cherry Tree Why She Blooms," "Lifting the Veil," "The Map Turtle"

A Confluence of Poems (Poems for Tributaries Everywhere), Eighth Annual Edith Chase Poetry Anthology, 2025: "The Chimney Swifts Are Back"

The Atlanta Review: "Geranium Red"

The Buddhist Poetry Review: "Looking Up From Down Here"

Calyx: "The Windfalls"

Cutleaf: "Not Lost," "The Present Tense," "When I press my cheek to the glass of heaven"

The Dodge: "I Have Been Gone too Long"

Flapper Press: "I Ask the Caterpillars About Meditation," "Red Bird"

Innisfree Poetry Review: "A Leap in Time," "On My Son's Fortieth Birthday"

Last Stanza: "After Reading Too Long About the Pandemic"

The MacGuffin: "Another Land War," "What It Means to Be Blessed"

Naugatuck River Review: "Home," "Knitting on Election Eve," "Old News"

Persimmon Tree: "The Valentine Month"

Poetry Breakfast: "Memory's Home"

Pine Mountain Sand and Gravel: "Divinity"

Sheila-na-gig online: "Mockery," "One Egg Cake," "Survivor," "Whistle"

Still the Journal: "The Willow Tree"

Still Points: "Sugar Cookies"

Southern Poetry Review: "Telling the Bees"

Terrain.org: "Fractals in November"

Weber, The Contemporary West: "Another Season," "The Cant Hook," "Nettles," "Two for a Penny or Free"

With Appreciation

The author would like to thank the Greenville Poets—David Garrison, Suzanne Kelley Garrison, Janet Irvin, Aimee Noel, and Myrna Stone—who have been supporting each others' work for over 40 years. This volume would not be possible without them and other friends in poetry, including Catherine Anderson, Pat Daneman, Susanna Lang, and Mary Jo Werthman White.

Contents

We Are Still Here, Amazed

It's a simple art this honey making,
if you know the recipe.

Memory's Home

—after "Salt and Feathers" by Katina Pastis Radwanski

Here is the land of remembered things—
memory's dark home—where the salt

of the earth is wedded to the sky.
Here is *salt on the tail of a memory,*

the language of childhood, nursery rhymes
and playground chants. Here is laughter

and adolescence, the mystery of old age.
Here are all things gone, yet present—

wind swept land shaped by the sea,
the little burr of the forget-me-not.

Never mind, the broken things,
the cities in ruin, love thrown aside,

those whom you will never see again.
In this space all things are reframed.

Here are the names of everyone
you have ever loved. Here is eternity

tangled in the sea grass, and just over
the horizon a place that we call *forever.*

Remembering the Way Home

Home

I show my mother an old picture of five girls
with their arms linked, and although she can
no longer tell you what day it is, she smiles
and says, *Oh, Easter, 1945, the war is over.*

The boys are coming home, coming from Japan,
Okinawa, and the Philippines. No more dancing
with other girls, or with flat-footed, 4F boys.
Soon there would be sugar and butter, new shoes,

kisses and weddings. *I am wearing my last pair
of silk stockings that your father sent from Hawaii.
We were so happy.* The girls are in flowered skirts,
but my mother is wearing a cream colored suit,

to compliment her curves. Cut on the bias
with a sculpted lapel, it is almost too stylish
for Kirksville, Missouri. *Where did you get the suit?*
I ask, and she replies, *If I'm wearing it, I made it.*

She made her wedding gown, regretted the purchase
of a headpiece, but there was no time! They had
their lives to catch up on. The ivory gown
was lost among many moves, but the cutlery

and the kitchenware that my father brought
home from the Navy, each piece labeled USN,
they used for a lifetime—mixing shortcake,
stirring the soup, buttering the biscuits

that came out of the oven so hot they were
impossible to hold. My father would laugh
as he tossed one from hand to hand,
saying, *It doesn't get any better than this!*

French Jubilee Medal

—Veterans Day, Covington, Ohio

The boys who landed in Normandy,
who swam ashore at Omaha, Juno,
and Gold with rifles over their heads,
and lucky pennies in their pockets…

I didn't do anything, they say. *I washed dishes,*
I drove a truck. . .

have come tonight, grey and bifocaled,
to receive medals sent by the people
of France, who still remember the beaches,
the bunkers, K-rations, and Hershey Bars.

I hid in a farmhouse and a grandmother
brought me a cup of milk.

Freshly shaved and smelling of Old Spice,
wearing coats they can no longer button,
the old soldiers have come for dinner
at the Am Vets Hall in Covington, Ohio.

I escorted refugees and body bags,
cleaned mine fields.

The Ladies Auxiliary has worked
all day, arranging plastic flowers,
cutting noodles, covering tables,
slicing store bought pies.

I carried a grenade launcher up a hill,
took out a tank.

The PA system is scratchy, but each
man rises as his name is called,
each does his best to explain—
I didn't do anything, they say.

*I cared for the wounded, until I was
wounded, and then others cared for me.*

Peaches and Cream

My grandmother never put sugar on her cereal,
although her grandkids looked forward
to that sugary goo at the bottom of the bowl.

She learned to like it that way during The War,
as if a teaspoon of sugar would bring her boys
home from Europe and the South Pacific,

along with the jar of drippings beside the stove
that she saved for their ammunition. That kind
of frugality kept her going, was handed down

to my father, who had a drawer for string
"too short to save." She wore house dresses until
they were beyond repair, turned them into aprons

worn until they were fit only for rags.
And yet, her pies were magnificent.
You can't be stingy with a pie, she said.

It takes a full quart of fruit and you want to save
a little sugar for the crust. By the time we came along,
there was butter and sugar and cream to spare.

When she said *peaches and cream,* she meant *cream*—
not low-fat, or even half and half, but the real stuff
that clung to the peaches and turned them into a dish

so redolent of home that even now, looking at the Breyers
label in the grocery, knowing I will be disappointed,
I choose Peaches and Cream to honor that kitchen

table with its oil cloth cover, the cream we poured
from a pitcher, and a heavy blue bowl with more
peaches than any child should be allowed to eat.

Divinity

I am standing on a chair next to the stove,
watching my mother make Divinity.
She spools the hot syrup into a cup of water,

pushes it into a ball, a process part alchemy,
part mystery, to a four year old who is not
allowed to stand on chairs except

when my father is away and then only
with caution to *get those size threes off that chair*
the moment we hear the car in the drive.

I have heard the stories, tales handed down
until they are family legends—an aunt scalded
by hot tomatoes, my own grandmother,

her hand wrapped in cold towels after a toddler
reached for the coffee pot. Still, my mother
lets me pull the chair closer to the bubbling pan

where I can see the hot syrup spatting the top
of the stove, safer she thinks than rules
she cannot enforce. Years later, my own children

curious at the stove's hot edge, I understand
my mother's solution to the problem, understand
my father's fear that made rules not to be broken.

It was my mother who taught me how to vent
the canner, handle the sharp knife, my father
who taught me how to put ice on the burn,

bandage the wound, he with his desire for safety,
she knowing that there is no safety until
you understand the danger.

Whistle

Try as I might, I never learned to whistle,
and so today when a cardinal calls from the hedge,
I open my Ipad and let it whistle back to him.

He answers, again and again, clear and ecstatic,
until my conscience bothers me. Who am I
to promise a happiness that isn't mine to give?

But now, I remember my mother sitting on the back step
of a house in Salina, Kansas, whistling to a cardinal
who is answering from the neighbor's new TV antenna.

It is 1957, and she is wearing a red halter top, and pedal
pushers that break at her knee. The cardinal sings,
prettee, prettee, prettee, and she answers with a warble

that encourages him to sing again and again. I am ten,
and I know that she is beautiful, dark hair pulled away
from her face, red bow at her neck, back bare to the waist.

Soon Eisenhower will pass by in a motorcade, waving
the way he does in newsreels on TV, and I will stand
on the curb and wave back in a memory that flickers

now in black and white. Surely, the grass was green,
the house a frosted stucco, my shirt bright with stars,
but today all I remember is the cardinal and my mother

sitting with her arms around her knees, mouth pursed
to imitate the red bird's happiness, and once again
prettee, prettee, repeated at the end of a summer's day.

In the Kitchen, 1956

At the breakfast table, my grandmother says,
I guess Lainey has gone off to have her baby.

My mother nods to show that she has heard,
and although I am still in grade school, I am

beginning to understand things that go unsaid.
I know that Lainey married, assuming her fiancé

was like her, and from listening at the pantry door
I know about other things as well—the stories

that women tell while baking bread, shelling peas.
I know that an infant was left on the minister's

front porch, and once a newborn was handed to
a young couple just as the carnival left town.

Years later, I think about my playmates at the end
of the street—beautiful girls with dark curly hair,

and I wonder if there were siblings that Lainey
did not bring home, babes that she left in the care

of other women. Today, there is no one that I dare
ask, my mother well into her eighties, her memory

fragile and the past so near that sometimes she
awakens with tears in her eyes, inconsolable,

even as I, her grown daughter, try to comfort her
as she explains, *I had that dream again—*

that my children were born with dark skin and
someone wanted to take them away from me.

Knitting on Election Eve

—November, 2020

My mother says she was born knowing how to knit.
Indeed, she knitted through classes, faculty meetings,
road trips, and most of our nation's armed conflicts.

Twisted stockinet during the War, followed by baby
clothes on size aught needles, and stretchy garter stitch
and basket weave for toddlers. But she didn't truly hit

her stride until the 60's, when she began a series of
"war sweaters." With one eye on the nightly news
and the other on her needles, she knitted through riots,

bombings, assassinations, and how many wars?
As our country lurched from one disaster to another,
she produced hats, scarves, sweaters and afghans

in intricate Aryan Isle surrounded by seed stitch and
ribbing so tight that it refused to budge regardless
of how wiggly the wearer. Even the dog, not a small dog,

mind you, had his own cabled coat with a ribbed neck.
We wore those garments like armor, like a promise
that things would get better if we could just remember

that every sweater is made from a single strand
of yarn, twisted and knotted into place. And so tonight,
on Election Eve, in a country unraveling at its own seams,

I turn on the evening news and in my mother's memory,
I cast on 164 stitches of arrowhead lace,
to honor the future and a baby who will arrive in April.

One Egg Cake

When the sewing machine choked on its own
bobbin and refused repair, or checkbooks
wouldn't balance,

my mother would turn her hands to the air
and say, *What we need now is a little*
one egg cake,

words so familiar that we knew intuitively
they had nothing to do with baking.
The phrase was a trope

for all of those moments when others might
find you wanting or unprepared.
Only once did she explain

that when she was a girl, she took berries
to an elderly aunt who suggested
that her young niece

might step into the kitchen and "make us
a little one egg cake." My mother,
only child, fond of music

and dancing, knew little about baking,
but the words stayed with her
for the rest of her life.

Through the years, many cakes passed
through her kitchen—angel foods
with seven minute icing,

rum cakes with pecans, and my father's
favorite, a hickory nut cake with
penuche frosting, made

from his mother's recipe and a secret
stash of hickory nuts. But no one
ever made a one egg cake.

Today, my mother is eating her favorite
gingerbread and trying to remember
my brother's name.

Charles, she says, and then shakes her head.
No, that's not right. George? she asks,
and an aide pats her on the arm—

That's right, sweetie, I knew you would get it!
Mother rolls her eyes to the ceiling,
and then turns to me to ask,

Did I ever teach you to make a one egg
cake? and in truth I can reply,
No, you never did.

Engineering

A chipmunk is sizing up the bird feeder, wondering
if he can shimmy his way inside the new squirrel baffle.
You can see him doing the math, plotting the angles.

Meanwhile, on TV, engineers are trying to cap an oil well
in the Gulf, using robotics and underwater photography
to measure their lack of progress, and Dad is in the garage

fussing over some engine he built from spare parts.
Maybe it needs belt dressing, or maybe I measured wrong?
I sketch the dimensions for him, tinker with the numbers,

but my high school math isn't helping much here, and Dad
reminds me that a college course in spherical trigonometry
kept him off the beaches during War II, made him a gunnery

officer in the South Pacific, which explains why he can't hear
me even now when I shout into his good ear, *Turn it off!*
The belt's too hot—I can smell the rubber burning!

He sits back on his heels, grousing, *What I need is a flexible,*
Lovejoy coupling, and I bet Frautchi could get me one,
except he's been dead for a couple of years now.

Outside the wind is stirring the sun in a magical sort of way,
so I try to imagine a séance in Frautchi's hardware store.
Surrounded with wrenches, sockets and appliances tagged

for repair, Arnold might come back just to fix Dad's motor.
He'd arrive with his hands on his hips and ask, *Geeze, Charlie,*
did you think this through, or did you just start building?

I can only imagine what he would say about the problem
in the Gulf. He'd lean against the counter and mutter
about everyone's parentage and lack of education.

The chipmunk, however, is doing well. I can see the pipe
shivering as he works the far edge of the pole, but Dad
is running a close second. Another yank on the starter

and the engine thrums into life, rattling tools and hinges.
Soon there will be blue smoke seeping under the door,
followed by the unmistakable acrid odor of success.

You Again

My father is wearing his leather apron, holding
a feral tomcat on his lap, while my mother pours

peroxide over the cat's ragged ears. Dad tries
to comfort him with a gloved hand, but a ripple

of distrust travels the length of his spine ahead
of every stroke. When they are finished, the cat

leans into my father's arm for just a moment,
eyes half closed, tail flicking, and then he bolts

for the door, rejecting the warmth of the kitchen,
the human touch. Dad watches as he disappears

into the bushes, over the riverbank. I check his
face to see if he is disappointed, but he is smiling.

He has no time for us, he says. We named him
anyway—called him Memory, because we thought

we would never see him again. But, he reappeared
that spring, after his wounds had healed and now

he had a younger cat in tow. He came for food,
a quick scratch behind one ear. He disappeared

again that fall, but the kitten stuck around,
the yellow one we named *So, It's You Again?*

Nettles

Now you know what nettles look like, Dad says,
as I rub cortisone onto my ankles.

He is an expert on prickly things, like how to
pull a thistle without going back for gloves.

He taught me how to get rid of a wasp's nest
(*Just don't!*) and how to smoke down a hive.

I read online about folk remedies for stinging
nettles—baking soda or saliva—too late for that.

Jewelweed and dock, applied like a salve, but
that would require another trip to the nettle patch.

I stick with the cortisone, which isn't helping
much, although the dog who dragged me

through the nettles is sound asleep on the sofa,
feet moving in some slow motion dream.

Just to show off, I read from Wikipedia about
medicinal uses for stinging nettles which can

be used for treating allergies, eczema and
joint pain, or dried and drunk as a tea, or

"cooked into healthful greens with onions
and bacon." After a long pause Dad says,

I don't think I've ever been that hungry, but
tell me again. . . why weren't you wearing socks?

Sugar Cookies

—for Jean

Every time I bite into a sugar cookie,
the kind Jean used to make, my teeth
sinking into that soft frosting,

I remember the afternoon that we sat on
her front step, eating cookies and watching
as dare-devil roofers hammered

shingles onto the steeple of the Green Street
Methodist Church. The men hung suspended
from cranes that lifted

them ever higher as they rappelled around
the steeple, their voices carrying so well
in the autumn air

that we could hear their happy banter as
they joked about doing the Lord's work.
The frosting on the cookies

was so sweet that it made my teeth ache.
Still, we watched all afternoon like children
at the circus, heads tilted skyward,

never doubting that the ropes would hold.
We never talked about the hard decisions
Jean needed to make—

the reason that I had come. We did talk
about the difference between courage
and bravery, as we passed

the cookies between us. We watched until
the street lights came on, and the men
were lowered to the ground.

The cookies were long gone, but as we stood
to brush the crumbs away, an Ohio sunset
bathed us all—steeple, crane,

people in the street—in such a tender light,
that in the end I think we decided bravery
would probably be enough.

Geranium Red

The geraniums that I rescued from an early snow
spent the winter in our sun room where they crowded
the doors and littered the floor well into May.

This morning when I carried them to the porch,
they left behind a trail of crimson petals the color
of my mother's favorite nail polish—Geranium Red,

a true fashion statement in the 40's, which caused
my father's friends to ask, *Is Charlie going to marry
that city girl who paints her nails?* Yes, he did—

you can see the polish in their wedding photos.
Although it is long before my time, red nail polish
still reminds me of the photos of Eleanor Kraus,

a fashionable New York matron who flew to Berlin
in 1939, clutching a handful of American visas, to rescue
fifty Jewish children whose families she had never met.

I think about those families who put their children
on a train with just a kiss on the cheek. *Smile,* they said,
Don't cry or wave goodbye. Don't frighten the children

or the guards will be suspicious. Today, the families
are all gone, of course, and the children aged,
but red nail polish is still my mother's favorite.

As I sweep the petals, I forgive the geraniums for the mess
they left behind, remembering how bravely they bloomed
all winter, and how they pressed their faces to the glass.

On My Son's 40th Birthday

My father and I are sharing a drink
while the birthday boy is lamenting
lost opportunities, his misspent youth,

but Dad and I honor another celebration—
three grandsons now, past the age
of military service, the draft and lottery.

No lump in the throat when your birthday
is called, no college deferments, no bodies
on beaches, fear of napalm, or sweethearts

left behind. My parents were engaged through-
out the War, my father refusing to marry,
for fear of leaving his wife a widow.

When her first grandson was born, my mother
pronounced him perfect in every way,
and then confessed she had hoped for a girl,

so we wouldn't have to worry about a draft.
Even now, well into her 90's, memory slipping,
she asks, *Who is this man who is running*

for President? Will he take us into a war?
I reassure her that our country is "at peace,"
and yet I know, somewhere, even today,

some mother has given birth to a son, and she is
afraid for him, afraid that someone has designs
on his beautiful limbs, his perfect sleeping face.

I pour a drink for all of the mothers who celebrate
this day, and another for my aging son, to remind
him that he still has his whole life ahead of him.

Another Land War

I.

How would I explain to my mother,
gone for several years now,

that there is another land war in Europe?
She would be saddened, but not surprised,

she who lived only for letters from Italy,
Japan and the Philippines, telling my father,

You must write every day, because a letter
that arrives on Friday tells me that you were

alive on Tuesday. Every morning she woke
to the static of the radio. Every night she sat,

with the newspaper in her lap, a map spread
across the supper table tracking the boys

who used to sit on their porch, cigarette
smoke rising around their faces.

On the map she circles Pompeii, Tokyo,
Manila, Pongo Pongo, Berlin. . . .

II.

And what would I tell Erika who clutched
her copy of *Gone with the Wind* while Allied

bombs fell around her in Vienna, who fled
Austria ahead of the Russian tanks?

She knew how to pack a suitcase, when
to take the pictures from their frames.

It is never too early to leave if you are walking,
she said, *and be sure of your destination*

if you are not. Lock the door if you are
an optimist; never mind if you are not.

Put on your winter coat, wear your best shoes.
Trust everything of importance to memory

and don't look back. Believe me—
you will never forget.

Walking Away

—for Vivian

I don't stop to remove
the pebble from my shoe,

because it reminds me of home—

one step to remember,
another to forget.

The Willow Tree
Or, Where To Lie Down

The willow tree my husband and I were married
under forty some years ago has come down
in last night's wind, although there was no wind.

It fell without a sound, almost unnoticed,
as if it simply chose where to lie down. Nothing
to betray it but leaf litter and a few broken limbs.

No scuffs along the eaves, the grape arbor still
standing, bee hives intact, although the lawn
is laced with a thousand green whippets.

Inside the house, my parents are wrapping up
their lives almost as quietly—no need for talk
when the memories are all your own.

We walk around the fallen canopy as if
it were holy. Something massive has
happened here without much acclaim.

Here the mystery of sunlight on leaves,
of cambium and phylum, where Wood Ducks
laid their eggs, taking a stand against

squirrels and raccoons. Here the lightning strike
that scarred the bark, reminding us of winter
nights when we lay in bed and listened

as the cold tested every joint and crevice,
claimed the choicest niche until we heard
the heartwood crack and boom. But today,

among the fallen, are the last pale blossoms
from the top of the tree, still tended by bees,
forever grateful for these spare blooms.

The Cant Hook

I

My brother puts a wedge under one end
of a 600 lb log that comes up to his waist.

He attaches a cant hook to the other end
and then leans into the handle.

The log shifts almost imperceptibly,
leaving a patch of torn grass behind.

We move the wedge, try again, readjust.
We guide it toward the congregation

of cut logs accumulating in the corner
of the lawn, just above the river bank,

logs so big we hesitate to send them crashing
over the incline. A few more corrections,

and we can roll it to where the others
have been stowed, waiting for the inevitable.

II

Inside the house, our parents are dying,
each of them making the slight adjustments,

compromises that get us through another day.
Yogurt poured into a cup, a spoon balanced

in someone else's hand, each rising a moment
of accomplishment measured against the inability

to recognize the time of day, the new face
at the door. Yes, a new face at the door. . .

someone so familiar that we are not surprised,
and yet, a new face at the door. Come in,

we say, but still they linger, welcome,
but not yet. Please wait here, we say,

and they oblige, while we adjust the bedclothes
say the things we are supposed to say.

Old News

My father puts his thumb next to the bark
of an aging stump and begins to count inward.

Here, he says, *is the winter that the ice came up*
over the bank—you remember that—and this is

the year when we moved to this house, and this
is when you and your brother were born and I

came back from the war. Here is that summer
there was no rain, and this is when my parents

were born. This tree was just a sapling, young
and green, when my people came to this place.

He smooths the stump with his palm, brushes
away the grit, stands where the tree once stood.

In his old age, my father began planting trees,
mowing around the volunteers, transplanting

them from the garden to replace the trees the city
considered too old, broken, or simply in the way.

A walnut grove sprang up next to the house.
Soon oaks and lindens lined the drive, and later

there were hickories which he scavenged from
the homestead in Missouri. He lived long enough

to see them shade the house, to foster generations
of squirrels and orioles. In his final days, he held

court at the end of the drive, telling the old stories
again and again. The neighbors came to remember,

and the trees leaned in to listen as the moon rose
over the lindens. And so today when I go out to talk

to the oaks, there is no need for conversation.
All news is old news, and there is nothing left to say.

Telling the Bees

When my father died, I stood in front of the hive
and by tradition said, *The beekeeper*
is dead; I am the new beekeeper.

I didn't know if that was a promise or a threat.
I wanted to say, *You can leave if you like,*
but we hope you will stay,

the same thing I wish I had said to my father,
although his choices were already made.
Two years later, bees are still coming and going

at the hive, although they have raised a new queen
after a brutal winter. What can we offer in return
for honey? Shelter from the wind, sugar water

in the Spring, medicine for pneumonia and mites?
Still, I feel like a thief as we calm them with smoke,
wave the workers aside with gloved hands,

find the queen deep in the hive, surrounded by
her keepers. Lifting the heavy, golden frames,
we choose only the ones they have capped.

We set new frames, install the baffles to keep
out beetles, and then weight the lid of the hive
with a stone to deter skunks and weasels,

or mice who might overwinter here. We step
back to watch as the workers regroup, return
to their familiar work. They set off on tangents

known to them and the sun, while we stand
motionless, still tethered to this place,
grateful they remember the way home.

You Will Fly Free

Lifting the Veil

Experiments indicate that bees have surprisingly rich inner worlds.
—Lars Chittka, *The Mind of a Bee*

In the darkness of the hive, 20,000 bees
are framing 100,000 hexagonal cells
so precise that they were once
considered a unit of measure,

while workers deep inside an almond
grove, saddlebags loaded with pollen,
take a last measure of the sun
before turning towards home.

Still, researchers insist on asking
the obvious—can bees replicate
a task, recognize faces, measure
distance, share joy, and distress?

I hope the bees are amused by it all—
as if the human umwelt was the only
perception in town? *What do you*
think being a bee is all about?

Inside the hive, they must trade
their own cautionary tales:
Beware the boy with a stick.
Avoid spiders and their webs,

and flowers so sticky and sweet
they will smother you in nectar.
But most of all, do not panic
when the keeper fills the hive

with smoke and you get caught
inside his hood. Stay calm,
the smoke will recede. He will
lift the veil and you will fly free.

The Windfalls

—for Marjorie, July 16, 2017

Our lover of taffeta and lace, slipped away
without notice on a perfect summer day—

sunlight glittering on the river, the lawn
a dizzying mix of sun and shadow,

and I am in the kitchen, cooking windfalls—
the little apricots that fell onto the drive.

I stir them into a golden slurry so fresh
and sweet they need no sugar.

And now the beekeeper arrives to marvel
at our forgotten hive, at the bees

that chose us, even when we failed
to prepare a space for them.

He lifts a frame, points to the queen,
raises his white veil and smiles.

Yes, I had hoped for a lucid moment,
a word or two, but there was only this,

and in the morning a praying mantis,
sleeping on my window sill.

I Ask the Cherry Tree Why She Blooms

The old cherry tree, battered by wind and age,
has bloomed again this spring, just as sweetly
as she did when she was young.

I see no signs of regret or nostalgia for years
gone by, but I know that she is counting.
ring by ring, as am I.

We wired the splintered trunk so long ago
that we can no longer find the scars.
Robins have made a claim

in the canopy, and squirrels are already
practicing their reach. I want to ask
how long the years can hold,

when the fruit will become more than
she can bear, but she has no time for me.
She has new blossoms

to attend to, fragile as baby's breath,
and Spring is still the bravest
season of the year.

My Mother's Necklace

The last time she removed
the gold necklace, she dropped it
into a blue bowl beside her bed,

an old habit, so familiar she didn't
remember releasing the clasp,
or even watch as the necklace

collapsed, link by link, upon itself.
She wore no jewelry after that,
no earrings, or rhinestone belts,

just her wedding rings which we
later set on the kitchen shelf.
The necklace remained pooled

in the bottom of the bowl, until I
picked it up one day, years later,
let the links reform themselves

one after another. I smoothed
the chain with my fingers, opened
the simple clasp, wore it myself

on special occasions, but now
I lay it carefully over a velvet rod,
not wanting those years to collapse

again upon themselves. The days
I wanted so desperately to forget,
I am now happy to remember.

A Leap in Time

—for Levin, who asked, If I become invisible, will time hold still?

Fifty is cold, my mother said, handing me
a sweater I did not want. Nothing prophetic

in her words, just a mother's timely remark.
And yet, the phrase became my reference point

regardless of where I lived. Fifty was cold in
North Carolina, Kansas, and Nebraska;

still cold when I moved to Texas and Tennessee.
Little did I know that words can alter time,

that the past can ride its way into the future,
like a burr clinging to the hem of your coat.

Never mind that I can no longer recall the town,
or if there was a school bus waiting at the curb.

But if memory falters, does it really matter?
Doesn't the present still unravel around us,

tugging at the past, pushing into the future?
Today, I remind my grandson that *fifty is cold*

and hand him a jacket he doesn't want to wear.
He grins, pulls it on anyway, and then spreads

his arms wide as he leaps from the porch, so
the wind can lift the coat away from his body,

carry him into that space between past and present
where he can slip, almost unseen, into thin air.

Synchronous Display

—Fourth of July, 2020

With the promise of fireworks in the distance,
we set up lawn chairs, decide to stay home.

The fireflies, however, are ignoring social distancing,
because signaling for a mate is essential—the life

and death work of each generation. My neighbor's son
obliges by standing on a picnic table to direct the display.

He raises his arms and *Boom*! the night explodes
as fireflies drop their sweet artillery over the lawn.

We applaud his effort while he prepares for an encore.
His girlfriend comes to stand behind him, kisses

him on the neck, lets her hands fall to his hips,
as he raises his arms for another crescendo of light.

Behind us, we can hear the fireworks along the river
as they pummel the evening air in concert with

our backyard display, holding us for just a moment
in that silence between light and its expectation.

I Ask the Caterpillars About Meditation

The caterpillars in the garden
have eaten all of the dill and
are moving onto the parsley.

Every morning I go out to ask
if they are ready for a hand into
the future, and every morning

they reply, *Just a bit longer. . .*
But nights are getting cold, and
I remind them that I've saved

a place for them to pass the winter,
suspended in chrysalis, protected
from mice and unseasonal warmth.

All I want in return is to ask
them how they fold in,
infinitely, upon themselves

and go into a meditation so deep
that time is no longer a constant.
But mostly, I want their advice

on how to return in the spring
as a changeling, where everything
is familiar—*the dizzying mix*

of sun and shadow, the breeze
that stirs the linden—and yet
nothing is ever quite the same.

The Chimney Swifts Are Back

The chimney swifts are back,
straight to this chimney
from some rooftop in Peru,

chittering their bright Peruvian
gibberish about storms on the coast
that blew them days off course.

They arrive at dawn, having flown
all night. I can see them coming
from far away, a slow, ragged line,

circling the house two, three times
before sliding down the chimney
so quickly that I lose count.

Two weeks overdue, I assumed
them lost, or fickle, finding
another rooftop more inviting.

Still they came, following
familiar landmarks—tracing
the curve of the Gulf, north

to the Mississippi, the Ohio,
and the Great Miami, where they
surely felt the pull of home,

resting perhaps on the Stillwater
Prairie before making the final
push to this small parcel of land

beside Spring Creek. Here they
will raise their young, and urge
them south again in the Fall,

pulled by the tilting of the planet,
and trusting a migratory map
that will not lead them astray.

The Map Turtle

The Map turtle riding in the backseat of my car
doesn't understand that I am taking her home.
She is pawing, rhythmically,

at the corner of her crate, just as she has been
doing for the last three months while her shell
re-grew under the pink epoxy

the rehab staff has applied. She is a hefty chunk,
the biggest book on my library shelf. She is
the unabridged OED,

all of Bullfinch's mythology. She is the best part
of the only creation myth that I can believe in,
for I have seen turtles rise

from an icy pond to fan their feet in the first thin
rays of sun. Together, we are looking for the place
where she was born,

that section of land that she knows better than any
other. I turn off the radio, concentrate on the map.
The news is always the same—

everyone trying to be somewhere else. But, tonight
I'm grateful to the intern who noted the mile marker
where she was found

and added this little sketch—three boulders on a tiny
beach where the water often meets the road. I park
the car, turn on the flashers,

and then balancing the crate on the guard rail, I swing
each leg over and lift the crate down to the creek bed.
When I lift the door,

she startles for just a moment, and then steps out,
turning her head left and right. She is making hard
decisions. I glance over my shoulder

to check on the car—it's a tight turn, a narrow road.
When I look down again she is gone. Simply gone.
I push aside the weeds,

the honeysuckle, but she is nowhere to be found.
I imagine a slight ripple in the water—once again,
she has returned to myth.

Mockery

The catbird is complaining about the cat
who is sitting under the honeysuckle
grousing about the catbird,

who has no nest to protect, who long ago
sent her fledglings into the air, but is still
full of epithets about the cat

who simply wants the bird to go elsewhere,
to stop announcing her presence
while she is hunting for chipmunks,

although by now every available rodent
has dug in for the evening or left for safer
territory where there are no catbirds,

and certainly no cats, while the two of them
mock each other as if this is a genuine dispute,
which may explain the cat's frustration

as the catbird, that dilettante, that charlatan,
that grey-capped mincing annoyance,
tries out new trills and voices.

It would be so easy for the catbird to simply
fly away, but no, she persists, bouncing from
one limb to another, meowing in that raspy,

cranky voice that sounds nothing like a cat,
if you are a cat, or too much like a cat
if you are a chipmunk or a critic

with an ear so discerning that now even
the cat can no longer sound like herself,
unless of course there is no catbird.

Homecoming

I drop six of my son's lucky coins into a paper bag
of milkweed seeds that I want to scatter along

the hedgerow, each coin a Japanese yen selected
for its heft and its uncanny ability to bring him

home from faraway places. I shake the bag hard,
hoping to separate the seeds from their floss.

Yet each time I open the bag to check my progress
a few volunteers drift away, riding little parachutes

they themselves have packed, banking on a gentle
breeze and a friendly landing on our foreign soil.

I could have scattered the seed with floss intact,
allowing it to drift into every tangled thicket,

but I am eager to give it a better chance to tether
itself to this place. When I am done, I rip a corner

of the bag and pour the seeds into my palm—
they make a hefty handful. I separate the coins

from the remaining floss, and then cast the seeds
like money into the wind, into the leafy mulch

of October, hoping that the earth will remember
them and welcome them home.

Fractals in November, or Why All Things Remain the Same

$z_{n+1} = z_n^2 + c$

I trace around the lobes of a red oak leaf,
noticing the two short nubs close to the stem,

and the next two that extend a bit further,
and then two more, like fingers pointing

in different directions, before it finishes up
with a self-important finial at the tip.

I move on to the maple's wide palm
and the yellow coin of the apricot.

Old botany lesson, pencil reminding me
of their differences, and what I know

about fractals, how these leaves, following
orders from under ground, practice

the only equations they know. And I compare
each as it mimics the tree from which it came—

the cathedral of the oak, the wide canopy
of the maple, the globe of the apricot—

these self-similarities, our only ways of knowing.
None of them thinks outside the equation,

and neither do I, as I trace around another leaf,
marveling that I, too, have nothing new to bring

to Spring and Fall, except this observation of me
observing a leaf and the tree from which it fell.

When I press my cheek to the glass of heaven,

I hope to be forgiven for my lack of faith
in the natural world.

Behind the mask of science, reason, myth,
there is forever another mask,

every intricacy slipping us clues, but never
the answer we want.

A bird lays an egg in a nest in a tree
that my father planted

from an acorn thirty years ago. It changes
everything—it changes nothing.

Inside the fruit a seed, inside the seed,
another tree planning

its next assault on Spring, complexity within
complexity—infinity nothing

more than another layer of uncertainty.
And yet, I have been told

that spiders dream, that flowers shiver
at a human touch,

that the cosmos can pulse and breathe
at a discernible pace.

The Present Tense

Afloat on a summer day, I can see it now,
how the present nudges us into the future,

the way my granddaughter's grey eyes
reflect her father's, or that age-old,

familiar glance my grandson gives me
from his keyboard. The future comes,

not in a rush, the way the dog brings
the sheep to the post, but how the cat

picks up her kittens one-by-one, by
the scruff of the neck, moving them

silently to another secret place,
just as mysterious as the present

but with a promise that there is more
to come, even as days grow shorter,

even as time makes its claim on us,
marks us in the long calendar of days,

that recognize the present as a moment
to be seen, a moment to be left behind.

We Are Still Here, Amazed

Mail Order Bees

When the post office calls at midnight
to say that Dad's bees have come in,
he slides a baton under the front seat.

It's not a safe neighborhood in the middle
of the night, although 10,000 bees
in a box should deter almost anyone.

We bring them home, freshen their water,
set them in the garage for the night.
By morning they have freed the queen

from her candy castle. We pour them
into a clean hive and soon everyone is
minding their manners, humming along.

We don't know when the queen made
her maiden flight, came back with enough
sperm to keep the hive producing.

We hope she found some nice local boys,
not the thugs from down river, the ones
that made the last hive turn mean.

We'll wait to see how the kids turn out,
but clearly these girls know there is
work to be done and get right to it.

If this hive becomes wild, we can always hope
for a workers' revolt, hope they will raise
another queen before booting the drones.

But, if anyone is planning a coup, we won't
know until late in the summer, and by then
there should be enough honey for everyone.

What It Means To Be Blessed

—It's a simple art this honey making,
if you know the recipe

When we lift the lid of the hive,
the abundance is clear, the frames
tight and swollen,

capped cells overlapping the aisles.
We crack the wax, pry the frames
apart as the bees,

smoked into stillness, lift lazily into
the air. We take only the honey
that they can spare,

replace the frames and seal the hive
against the coming cold, as the bees,
still airborne, wait

for the hive to close, for the darkness
that makes the bright honey possible.
We uncap the frames

with a heated knife, and soon we are
pouring new honey into mason
jars, the liquid so viscous,

so heavy, that it overflows the rim,
runs down my sticky fingers,
onto the kitchen tray.

There's nothing to do but put the jar
down into the golden puddle
thickening below.

Nothing to do but lick my fingers
and laugh, and in that moment
I know I am blessed,

will always be blessed, and honey
fills my mouth with its wild,
indescribable sweetness.

Not Lost

The GPS thinks I am lost on these country roads,
and it may be right, but I have been this way
before and am counting

on landmarks to show me the way, even as
the GPS voice recalculates my every turn.
Soon, I will pass

a family cemetery with its single broken yew.
I've always wanted to stop, but not today.
Today Beth has invited me

to come see the newborn lambs. It has been
a hard winter, with losses still too fresh
to be named.

Come see that the world is still with us,
she says, even though others may
have left it behind.

Another mile, and I pass the Amish meeting
house with its horse-drawn buggies
tied up along the fence.

But I am going farther—past the Stillwater
Prairie, turning onto a twisted road,
past a stone church

built on land too rocky to be grazed, suited
only for steeples and tombstones.
And now, as I turn

onto a graveled lane. I can hear the long,
wavering cry of ewes and their lambs.
Baa, and *baa,* and *baa,*

they say, repeating the only words they need
to know—*I am here; I am not lost,*
and *I belong to you.*

After reading too long about the pandemic. . . .

I go out to see what the frost has spared,
here late in May.

The seedlings I covered with an old T-shirt
and the new dogwood

I slipped into a pillow case look stunned, but ok.
The peonies, however,

break off in my hand like snapped asparagus.
The tender leaves

on the Chinese maple hang limp, but the oak
must have some antifreeze

against such things; its catkins tangle in my hair.
I stretch to see a nest tucked

under the eaves where a mother robin sat all night,
tight as a pot on a stove.

But today, four blue eggs, the color of heaven, lie
abandoned in the cold.

Soon I will check on the blue bird house, where
a family of sparrows moved in

two weeks ago. I didn't have the heart to evict them,
to wait for tardy bluebirds.

Now I am glad to see the little squatters are thriving,
small mouths opening, hungry

for whatever Spring has to offer, and for any face
that appears at their door.

Eden

Memorial Day at the cemetery,
and among the tombstones

a little girl named Eden
is stomping in the puddles

left by last night's rain.
Her shoes are sodden;

her skirt and face
are flecked with mud.

She is laughing so hard
she can barely breathe.

I think she is the happiest
child I have ever seen.

I Have Been Gone Too Long

I pull into the driveway late at night
and can smell the tang of peaches
rotting beside the garage.

It's almost August and Red Havens
ripen in July. I can imagine the mush
beneath the tree attracting

bees and wasps. The neighbors have yet
to complain, but they will get another
chance in September

when the apples begin to fall, their fusty
spice the odor of Autumn. There will
be yellow jackets drunk

on fermented fruit and squirrels so overfed
they take two bites of a perfect apple
before letting it drop.

So be it. I remind myself that the tree
has more interest in its seed than in
all of this fruit,

so carefully cultivated to lure us home.
And now I can't remember why
I have been gone so long.

What could need tending more in July
than this tree overburdened
with its own fruit?

And tomorrow I will bite into a peach
so sweet and fragrant that I can't
remember my own name.

Calling the Sparrows by Name

Every spring I vow to learn the names
of the sparrows, their brown rumps
such a common sight at my feeder.

I have never bothered with distinctions,
lumping them all together as omnipresent
twittering chumps, never picky about seed,

content to nest in any tight or prickly space.
I begin to catalog them—the House Sparrow
with his small black bib; the Fox, Sage and

Savannah sparrows with streaked breasts.
It takes patience, binoculars and a good book.
I'll admit that my ear is not good enough

to distinguish between the Song Sparrow and
and Vesper Sparrow whose song begins
with *two longer slurred introductory notes.*

The book struggles with synonyms for brown—
rusty, chestnut, dingy. Early in June, there is
other work to do—tomatoes to be staked,

beans replanted; robins are eating cherries
I intended for pies. By the time I get back
to the book, Chipping Sparrows have lined

their fledglings up next to the feeder. I move on
to easier birds—cardinals and jays. Who cares
if they are common east or west of the Mississippi?

I throw more seed into the feeder, put my feet up
on the table. The important thing is that no one
goes to bed hungry. Everyone gets fed.

Another Season

So, here are the seeds I carried
in my pocket all winter long,

the ones I intended to give to you.

Too late now for that small gesture,
for the hope that you might live

another summer to watch the children

pedal their bikes down the drive, to water
the Lantana, or pinch back the marigolds

we carried home in paper cups.

And now this sadness, like another person
in the room. Come in, we say. Please

ignore the wading pool, the children's toys.

Have a seat, here, on the porch and we'll
pretend you are just passing through,

that you do not intend to stay.

Can I bring you something to drink?
The children have Kool Aid in their cups,

which explains the stains on their shirts,

but not the Christmas flag, celebrating
the snow that they love so much

they could not bear to take it down.

Now another season lays claim
to their affection, so maybe they will

not notice if you decide to leave.

Here, take these seeds, put them
in this tray. Let's see if they grow,

or if they simply slip away.

Holding On

At the cemetery, he picks up a stone
and puts it in his pocket.

A month from now he won't remember
where it came from,

but never mind, he knows the weight
of it in his hand,

knows that he belongs to this place.
He touches it often,

reminds himself that he did something
in honor of a memory

he can no longer retrieve. In the end,
maybe that will suffice

for all of us—the thought, the action,
the stillness afterwards

that some might call grief, the loss
so universal

that it needs no name or stone
to anchor it to a place.

Two for a Penny or Free

Children are at the door selling buckeyes,
Two for a penny or free. They are beautiful—

fresh from the pod, that tender mahogany
that only September can supply.

I give each child a dollar, buy the whole stash
and then pocket a couple for good luck and

explain that I am going to toss them over
the riverbank and hope squirrels will help me

plant a buckeye forest. I describe the trees—
fingers waving in the sun, blossoms stacked

like candelabra each spring, and hummingbirds
delirious at their good fortune. But one little boy

is having seller's remorse. I can see him weighing
his choices—the cost of beauty versus its potential.

His chin is puckered, his eyes clouded by concerns
that he is much too young to consider.

I want to tell him to choose beauty every time,
to have no regrets even as he gives it away.

But now his friends are tugging at his sleeve,
laughing about how to spend their money,

and now they are dancing down the driveway,
empty buckets swinging from their arms.

This Cold Harvest

I look up expecting to see a splash
of sunlight on a rainy day,
but there is only this:

the yellow leaves of the hickory tree,
lit from below, incandescent
against a sodden sky,

and for just a moment, as the planet
tilts toward winter, it is possible
to believe in eternity.

This morning, after the first hard freeze,
I go out to pick persimmons
ripening in the cold.

I remember Persephone's dark bargain
made in order to keep
the earth alive.

I thank her again for this cold harvest,
sweetened now by frost, but still,
so astringent on the tongue.

Red Bird

The cardinal that I rescued from a snow bank
is now proselytizing from the top of the maple.

I hope he is mentioning the warmth of the house,
the fancy new birdfeeder with sunflower seed

and the heated water bowl on the patio.
I suspect he is talking mostly about himself,

like most of the converts that I have met,
as if their revelations might be passed on

like a simple communion, since none of us can
depend upon being gob-smacked by a window,

or expect a warming hand to lift us from the cold.
We have to make do with whatever falls our way.

And yet, today I held a red bird in my hand,
feathers askew, topknot blown to one side,

brighter than a valentine taped to the closet door.
In truth, I could have held him all day, made him

a familiar at my window sill. But I know
he should be singing for his mate, advertising

his prowess, promising to defend their nest.
I hope she will not find him wanting, can warm

to his exuberance, is not offended by his urgency,
or the new longing in his song that only I can hear.

March

The snowflakes
riding on the dog's
dark ruff
have made
an easy descent
from 8,000 feet,
edges crisp,
facets intact,
ribs and rods
distinct,
nothing like
the icy grit
that fell
two days ago,
travel-worn
columns,
needles rimed
with ice.

I would like
to call
this new snow
a touch
of spring,
a promise
that March
will not hold
grudges,
but I have seen
snow in April,
killing frost
in May,
and I have held
frozen blossoms
in my hands,

felt the petals
flake away
and fall,
like this snow,
to the ground.

J.T. Tibbs

The orange cat we rescued from the snow
after a winter storm soon became a house pet.

My mother named him for a red haired boy
in her class too shy to ask her for a date.

He was the only pet to earn a seat at the Sunday
table, because his manners were impeccable.

A tap on the wrist and you knew the next morsel
was meant for him, unlike the dogs who drooled

on knees and moaned about the injustice of it all.
Somehow, living in the wild had tamed him,

adversity giving him silent lessons in courtesy.
He never hissed at the dogs, stole the butter,

brought down the curtains. We never knew
his history and so, like all of us, he became

the hero in untold stories. Never mind the cold,
bitter nights, the mornings he woke to fear.

He has earned this place at the table where
the only blessing is the gift of belonging.

What Dead Fathers Do

Five inches of snow with more to come.
I pull on work gloves and go out to start
the aging blower that Dad bought
at an estate sale years ago.

Gone for almost two years now, he is still
full of advice: "First, put up your hood,
unless you want snow down your neck.
You put STABIL in the tank, didn't you?

We won't use Quick Start unless we need it.
Put the key in the ignition and turn it.
Pull out the choke, and then prime it
three times and wait. The bulb is old,

getting brittle, so push hard. Are those
the best boots that you own? OK, now pull
the cord and it ought to start right up.
There! Just like that!" Blue smoke circles

the drive and the motor roars its approval.
"Here, take my gloves," Dad says, "Those
don't look very warm," and then he goes back
to doing whatever it is that dead fathers do,

but I know the ritual: clear the drive, then go
across the street and do Betty's also. She doesn't
get out much, but we can't have her snowed in.
Don't forget the sidewalk or the city will be mad

at us, and then go a bit farther, just around
the corner, so the neighbors will know
that Dad and I got the blower running while
they were still in slippers, sipping coffee.

The Valentine Month

—for Henry

Thirty-four degrees, and the falling snow
turns to slush before it can hit the ground.

The dog comes in so wet and muddy
that I don't notice at first the faint odor

of skunk which flavors everything in February,
their mating season. The muck between

the dog's toes is a perfect marriage of ice
and rain and the sludge of an empty corn field

where he loves to hunt for small amorous
things in this, the Valentine month.

He luxuriates in the towel rubbed the length
of his spine, but reminds us *not* to touch his feet!

How easily spring nudges us into the present—
the smell of a wet dog almost inviting, intimate

in a grungy sort of way, if I were not so concerned
about the carpeting and fat muddy tracks.

What can this month possibly know about spring,
about love? Too early for vernal pools, too late

to caution the apricot about blooming so soon.
I've read the weather report, threatened

the peach trees, reminding them a late freeze
can drop little peaches like velvet buttons.

Love stirs nevertheless, and how glorious it is
to be towel dried, to be rubbed behind the ears,

to know that there is more to come, to know
that February is only the beginning.

Looking Up From Down Here

I am sleeping on the floor tonight to comfort
an old dog who can no longer make the leap
onto the bed,

old friend who should not be left alone tonight
of all nights. His big soft feet smell green
from the pasture,

and his breath comes in slow puffs of air
that make his cheeks flair. I have made
a pallet for myself,

but I am beginning to envy him his cushy
pillows. Looking up from down here,
I can see now

how everything fits together—here the repair
my father made on an antique table, and
above it hangs

my mother's crystal chandelier which I forgot
to dust before this holiday. Still, it sparkles
in the moonlight,

like a constellation waiting to be named.
I close my eyes and imagine the guest room
directly above,

where family sleeps in a big mahogany bed
and above them the tall attic with dusty
rafters where

we have stored all of our childhood memories.
But now I'm on the roof, and I'm not a bit
surprised to see

that the old dog has come with me. We watch
as boats slip down the river, and neighbors'
lights wink out, one by one.

Tomorrow there will be guests in the house,
but tonight it is just Orion and Canus Major
knocking at the door,

and I have grown so accustomed to this bed
on the floor, that I will wait for someone else
to rise and let them in.

Survivor

The pine tree that I rescued
from a crack in the sidewalk

is now twelve feet tall.
We planted it in your yard

the summer you began chemo.
I want you to know

that last year it dropped
its first pine cones

and this year it hosts
a nest of robins.

Wherever you have gone,
we are still here, amazed

by the little peach trees
that grow from seeds

planted by an ambitious
generation of squirrels.

The iris did not bloom
this year, but the peonies,

those aging ladies in pink
negligees, were beautiful.

I have not trimmed the lilacs
as I promised, but I will

once the blossoms have fallen.
In the meantime, all I can say

is that we are doing our best
to live a life worth dying for.

About the Author

Cathryn Essinger is the author of five previous books of poetry—most recently *The Apricot and the Moon* and *Wings, Or Does the Caterpillar Dream of Flight?* both from Dos Madres Press. *My Dog Does Not Read Plato* was published by Main Street Rag along with *What I Know About Innocence* which includes a video poem, *Dark Flower*, by her son Dave Essinger. Her first book, *A Desk in the Elephant House,* won the Walt McDonald First Book Award from Texas Tech University Press. Her poems have appeared in *Poetry, The Southern Review, The New England Review, Ecotone, Terrain.org, Rattle, The MacGuffin,* and other journals. They have been nominated for Pushcarts and Best of the Net, featured on *The Writer's Almanac,* and reprinted in *American Life in Poetry*. She lives in Troy, Ohio, where she raises butterflies and tries to live up to her dog and cat's extravagant expectations.

S
Sheila-Na-Gig Editions

www.ingramcontent.com/pod-product-compliance
Ingram Content Group UK Ltd.
Pitfield, Milton Keynes, MK11 3LW, UK
UKHW042013190726
13854UKWH00005B/2268